AROUND
BULKINGTON
IN OLD PHOTOGRAPHS
WITH ANSTY AND SHILTON

BULKINGTON TOWERS, C. 1930. An odd juxtaposition of parish church tower, now well into its fifth century, and the water tower which did not last fifty years. It was built in 1927 under the watchful eye of John Flowerdew.

AROUND
BULKINGTON
IN OLD PHOTOGRAPHS
WITH ANSTY AND SHILTON

COLLECTED BY
JOHN BURTON

ALAN SUTTON

Alan Sutton Publishing Limited
Phoenix Mill · Far Thrupp · Stroud · Gloucestershire

First Published 1990

British Library Cataloguing in Publication Data

Around Bulkington in old photographs with Ansty and Shilton.
1. Warwickshire, Bulkington. History.
I. Burton, John *1943–*
942.483

ISBN 0-86299-692-9

Front Cover Illustration:
CHURCH STREET, BULKINGTON, in 1905.

Typeset in 9/10 Korinna.
Typesetting and origination by
Alan Sutton Publishing Limited.
Printed in Great Britain by
Dotesios Printers Limited.

CONTENTS

For May Dawkins and Mary Goodland, with affection and thanks. Without them this would be an exceedingly slim volume.

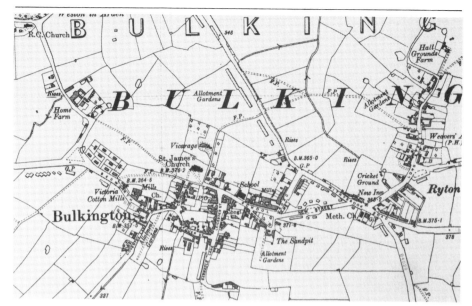

BULKINGTON in the 1920s, showing the original shape of the village, and distant Ryton. Reproduced by kind permission of Ordnance Survey.

INTRODUCTION

Like most villages in England, Bulkington has a long history. A mention in Domesday (1086) clearly indicates an existing settlement, and no doubt through the centuries inhabitants struggled hard to produce sufficient food to exist, as they laboured and toiled in the open fields of the villages. That struggle remains hidden since cameras were not around to record it. Nevertheless, aerial photography shows some of Bulkington's medieval strips on the open land adjacent to the church, and other traces exist, and have been photographed, in Shilton Lane and in Ansty.

The enclosure acts changed life for residents. One result was an increasing number of farms, and farmhouses, and they certainly existed long enough to be photographed. Indeed, at one time Chequer Street seems largely to have consisted of farms – and pubs.

In Bulkington, to a lesser extent Shilton and Ansty, and to a greater extent Ryton, another development was taking place concomitant with enclosure. Ribbon weaving became established in the area, and soon became the largest employer. Usually whole families were involved since schools were primitive and children were expected to work from a young age. There were always jobs for them associated with the loom. Bulkington and Ryton seem to have had a majority of hand looms – domestic machines which stood in a room downstairs. There were some purpose-built top shops with a more businesslike approach to organizing labour, but they were the exception. In Coventry and Bedworth, by contrast, much bigger factories were established.

From 1751 to 1851 the population of Bulkington trebled and many of the dwellings whose photographs appear in this book were built during the first half of the nineteenth century. They are often distinguished by a chequered brickwork. Indeed, the villages were almost completely rebuilt and enlarged (particularly Ryton) in those years and the Bulkington which present inhabitants remember was not much more than 100 to 150 years old, though its roads and tracks were the old agricultural ones, and some much older buildings remained. No doubt inhabitants in 1850 bemoaned the new Bulkington, just as many do today.

The rigours of farming and the terrible vicissitudes of ribbon weaving made life hard after 1860. The population fell, and many photographs here show a village which barely kept poverty at bay, right up until the last war. It was never a traditionally picturesque village, whatever that is, but it seems to have had a strong sense of identity and cohesion which is evident from some of the 'social' photographs.

In recent, post-war years the village has lost its uniqueness, and most of its buildings. While replacement is clearly necessary, Bulkington has been ill-served by much rebuilding of the last thirty years, and the old photographs serve to emphasize the wrongness of scale and proportion in much of Leicester Street, for instance. More recently, the conversion of Weston Hall Stables and the new development in Church Street show a greater sensitivity to the visual appearance of the village, and offer hope for the future. Yet it seems a sad sign of the times that a village as large as this is unable to keep open its parish hall, a building which symbolically carries within it so much of the community history of Bulkington.

Much of the material in the book came directly from local residents at the time of the village exhibition in 1981. My small part in that very successful event was to copy photographs which the indefatigable May Dawkins borrowed from local residents. We were thus able to enlarge pictures to a size suitable for display and return the precious originals.

Meanwhile, I have added to that large nucleus during the 1980s and at least once a year have been able to 'feed back' to Bulkington, through slide shows and talks, its own pictures. At one of these talks, in early 1988, Mary Goodland responded to the notion of collecting and copying old photographs of the village she and her husband had recently moved to, Ansty. There followed several months of enjoyable discussions with Ansty and Shilton residents which culminated in a slide show in Ansty in November 1988.

Without Mary's dedicated work, one quarter of the book would not be here. Without May's, a decade ago, great chunks of the Bulkington section would not be here. It is, in a real sense, their book, though the faults, of course, are all mine.

Bulkington Station to Church Street

BULKINGTON STATION in Edwardian times. Three ladies and two railway employees pose for the photographer. The architecture speaks of the confidence and vigour of Victorian railway companies.

STATION MASTER TURNER and one of his staff. They are standing to the right of the lady on the right in the picture above. They are wearing LNWR uniforms and the picture is earlier than 1909, since Mr Turner retired that year.

BULKINGTON STATION, perhaps in the 1950s. It shows the island platform, which has disappeared in the lower picture. The station was not a Beeching victim, having closed some time before.

BULKINGTON STATION, looking sadly in need of attention, c. 1965. Electrification had been installed. The Trent Valley line remains an important link in the country's rail system, even though trains no longer stop at this outpost on the western edge of the village. The station building remains as a private house.

THE BULL RING, C. 1930. This is the junction of Weston Lane and Bedworth Road. The open grass now has trees and is attractive, especially in spring. The council houses had not long been built when this picture was taken and they stood in a no man's land between the village and Weston.

WESTON LANE, 1950s. The Catholic church is just visible on the left, but Weston Hall is completely hidden behind the distant trees. Weston was predominantly a farming community with the Hall at its centre.

WESTON HALL, c. 1907. One of F.R. Jones's less successful pictures, but despite the size and age of the house very few early photographs of it have surfaced. An imposing building with much sixteenth and seventeenth-century original work, it was extensively altered in the 1890s.

WESTON HALL STABLES. Derelict for many years until the mid-1980s when they were converted into lovely houses, sharing the communal front shown here. The picture shows them in 1982.

ARDEN LODGE, WESTON. This fine building stands in Mill Lane, opposite the stables (see p. 13). Considerably altered and extended, it is now an old people's residence, but was originally a farm. Mary Ashmore's family farmed there for a while before the First World War. Sam Record was there in 1914.

WESTON HILL FARM lies behind these houses, now replaced by one large modern one. This snow scene has great charm. The houses were opposite the Weston Lane junction with Nuneaton Road.

FARM WORKERS at Warner's Farm, Weston Hill, later Farndon's Farm. The picture was taken about 1900. The man with the pitchfork was a shepherd, William Rollaston.

THE BULL RING, again, after the detour to Weston. This view looks towards the village. The church tower is visible between the houses. Taken about 1930.

15

VIEW FROM CHURCH TOWER, 1950s. Looking west, towards Bedworth. The Bedworth water tower, Newdigate colliery and Nicholas Chamberlaine school are all visible. It shows the area before the School Road extension went across the recreation ground, along the line of the path.

VICTORIA COTTON MILLS, Bedworth Road. These stood where the old people's complex now is, between the main road and Bedworth Close. On the right can just be seen part of Record's farm. Behind the Mills the top of the water tower can be seen.

SHOP AND BAKERY IN BEDWORTH ROAD, 1930s, now demolished. It stood on the north side of the road, a few yards to the left of the present doctors' surgery. Typically there was a line of houses behind, at right angles to the road. This one was known locally as Ranters Row. The little chapel (see p. 24) was at the top of the row.

COTTAGES IN BEDWORTH CLOSE, formerly Road, 1982. Demolished and now a doctors' surgery. The shop on p. 17 was to the left of these. The farm pictured below stood opposite.

HOME FARM, Record's Farm. Two other farms were called Home, but not at the same time. The house and buildings occupied the corner site of Coventry Road and Bedworth Road (see p. 20). The front was at right angles to the road and looked towards Bedworth. The patterned brickwork was typical of its early nineteenth-century period all over North Warwickshire.

HOME FARM, rear, showing part of the yard. The left-hand side is the rear of the building shown on p. 18. The right-hand part was adjacent to Bedworth Road and was linked to the stables by an older building.

STABLING AND FARMYARD, enclosing the farm and following the road junction of Bedworth and Coventry Roads. The chimneys belong to Ashleys' building which stood almost opposite the farm, at the top of Coventry Road.

AN AGED BULKINGTON RESIDENT, sitting in the garden of Home Farm. She was Miss Jemima Orton, originally from Shilton. The picture was taken a few months before she died in 1938. She was in her eighties.

THE JUNCTION OF COVENTRY ROAD, Bedworth Road and Chequer Street. The farm buildings came right to the corner and suffered many knocks from errant vehicles. Ashleys' house and workshop is on the right. Everything in this picture has gone.

OVENTRY ROAD, 1907. The fixed point is the bow-fronted line of houses on the left. They are :ill there. The thatched cottage at right angles to the road has been removed as far back as 1e chimney. Ashleys' has gone. On the right were allotments, now houses.

OVENTRY ROAD 1950s. A similar view but there are many changes to examine. A modern iew shows even more changes.

EDWIN ASHLEY, when an old man, in the garden of his house (below). The top of the water tower is visible behind him.

ASHLEY RESIDENCE, top of Coventry Road, now demolished for the extension of the road. Several generations of builders and craftsmen have worked in the village, and do so still.

WORKSHOP INTERIOR at Ashley's. This was the building on the right of the house. This bookcase and bureau was made in the workshop, with a high degree of skill.

EDWIN ASHLEY
(Late JOHN COTTON),

CARRIAGE, CART, AND VAN
—— BUILDER, ——

BEDWORTH ROAD,
BULKINGTON.

ALSO,

Builder & Contractor.
ESTABLISHED 1830.

AN ASHLEY ADVERTISEMENT from a local booklet and calendar for 1908. The firm has been in the village for 160 years, with an unrivalled reputation for quality.

THE FINAL SERVICE at Bulkington Methodist Church, 12 October, 1960. After 110 years the building was unsafe and the closing service was held outside. The chapel was only a few yards from Ashleys'.

CHEQUER STREET, 1907. There are allotments on the right, which run down Coventry Road (or Lane at that time). The building on the right is Villa Farm (see p. 32), and Church Street runs off to the left where the road curves out of the picture beyond the bicycle.

CHURCH STREET, from the Church Tower, 1950s. Containing some very old buildings, those in the foreground disappeared under the new road. Villa Farm is behind the tree at the top of the picture. Happily the tree remains. The building half way down the left side of the picture, with its long roof sloping towards us, belonged to Mr Farndon. It is very old indeed, with some massive roof beams.

THE INTERIOR OF A WORKSHOP in Church Street, the building with the sloping roof referred to above.

THE CROWN INN
BULKINGTON.

FREDERICK BENN   -   -   -   Proprieto₁

BRUNT, BUCKNALL & Co.'s INDIA PALE ALE & SPECIAL STOU

CELEBRATED ALES AND STOUT.

━━━━ Good Accommodation for Cyclists. ━━━━

AN ADVERTISEMENT FOR THE CROWN INN, 1907. This pub was ideally placed on a corner and served the cheek-by-jowl inhabitants of this part of the village. It is the bow-windowed building on the left in the picture below.

CHURCH STREET, 1905. A superb example of a postcard by F.R. Jones of Nuneaton. All the buildings on the right are still there and some are older than their brickwork suggests. James Wright was the publican at the Crown when the picture was taken.

CHURCH STREET, 1950s, showing the extension to the Crown in the foreground. A further extension at the back is visible behind the men in the picture below.

THE CROWN INN, 1950s, showing proud members of the darts and dominoes team with their trophies. On the front row, seated extreme right, is the landlord at the time, Bill Wagstaff.

A COTTAGE IN CHURCH STREET. One of Bulkington's oldest buildings, probably there by 1600, this picture shows the sorry state into which it had fallen. Fortunately the present owners have lovingly and carefully restored this listed building, and won an award for doing so.

THE PARISH CHURCH OF ST JAMES, Bulkington. A very fine building with many interesting features. Peter Wyman's booklet, or the Victoria County History provide more detail than can be attempted here.

CHURCH STREET CHILDREN, looking slightly self-conscious, not to say apprehensive. The picture dates from the late 1940s or early '50s. The boy on the left is one of the Hinde family.

A CHURCH WALK ON SERMONS SUNDAY returning down Church Street. The children carry gifts of flowers and eggs. On the left is Ken Neale, head of the local school (and born in Church Street); next are church wardens Reg Green and Will Bason and on the right is Revd Dingley.

CHURCH STREET. Many of us growing up after the war have fond memories of tricycles. Much of Bulkington had the sort of paving and outbuildings shown in this picture and it shows the general poverty of agricultural villages after the depressed years of the 1920s and '30s. The Hinde grandparents brought up three grandchildren, including this young man, proud of his trike.

Chequer Street to Arden Road

VILLA FARM, Chequer Street. Not strictly a farmhouse, more a very fine residence for Mr Dewis who owned the Victoria Mills (see p. 16). There was land with it which at one time was farmed for Mr Dewis by the Records. On the site now is a single-storey Health Centre.

CHEQUER STREET, 1907. Photographer Ernest Ratledge stood in Church Street to take this. The curve in the road remains, with the Working Men's Club on the left and Villa Crescent leading down past the end of the wall. On the left was Hickinbottom's sweet shop and further down was the first chemist's shop in Bulkington.

THE POPLARS, Chequer Street in 1917. The barn appears to have lost its thatch by 1917 when the farm was sold.

THE BARN AT THE POPLARS, 1950s. In the first post-war town and country planning act survey this barn was listed Grade III. Sadly, that did not prevent its demolition to make way for a garage.

Particulars.

NOTE.—Lots 1, 2, 3, 4 and 5 are situate in the Village of Bulkington, ⅓ mile from Bulkington Station (L. & N.-W.R.), 4 miles from Nuneaton, 6 from Coventry, and 10 from Rugby.

LOT 1.

(Coloured Green on Plan).

THE EXCEEDINGLY VALUABLE

FEEDING AND DAIRY FARM,

known as

"THE POPLARS,"

BULKINGTON,

comprising about

102 Acres 3 Roods 5 Perches.

THE PICTURESQUE OLD FASHIONED RESIDENCE,

occupying an attractive position in the village, is in excellent order, substantially brick built with cement facings and tiled gabled roof, and contains :—**On the Ground Floor** : Drawing Room, Dining Room, Dairy, Kitchen with modern Range, Cellar, Wash-house with copper and sink. **On the First Floor** : Six Bedrooms. **Adjoining** : Yard with cooling-house, Out-offices, Flower and Kitchen Gardens.

CAPITAL FARM BUILDINGS,

including Brick, Half-timbered and Corrugated Range of Covered Gateway Entrance, Barn and Stabling for 6 horses with Loft over ; Brick and Tiled Ranges of 3 Pigsties, Cowhouses for 28, Hay Pen, 3 Loose Boxes ; Stock Yard ; Brick and Corrugated Range of Mixing-house with Loft over, Trap House, 3-bay Wagon Hovel and Loft over ; Lean-to Timber and Corrugated Trap House and Fowl House. In Field No. 538 on Plan is a very useful 4-bay Brick and Tiled Hovel, Loose Box, and Yard.

NOTE.—The Dutch Barn belongs to the Tenant, and is to be taken over by the Landlord at the end of the Tenancy.

Now let to Mr. C. F. Woodward at an apportioned rental of

Per £190 Annum.

3

AUCTION PARTICULARS for The Poplars. The details show how large the farm was, right in the centre of the village. The auction was held at the Newdegate Arms, Nuneaton on 11 September 1917.

JAMES EVANS, dairy farmer, outside The Poplars, where he was a tenant before 1910. It is a delightful picture.

A PIGEON
SHOOTING

WILL TAKE PLACE

ON MONDAY, JANUARY 19, 1857,

AT MR. EDWARD FLETCHER'S, OLD CHEQUERS, BULKINGTON,

FOR A FAT PIG,

Twelve Score, by 14 Subscribers at Ten Shillings each, ⅞ gauge Guns, 21 yards rise, 3 birds each, 1⅛ oz of Shot, 80 yards boundary.

NO MEMBER ALLOWED TO SHOOT FOR MORE THAN TWO TICKETS.

SHOOTING TO COMMENCE AT ELEVEN O'CLOCK.

PRINTED BY W. J. PEPPER, STATIONER, ETC., CROSS CHEAPING, COVENTRY.

A HAND BILL for one of many events staged at the Old Chequers over the years. This dates from 1857. It may well be that the fat pig would have been supplied by the farm next door.

CHEQUER STREET, C. 1905. The 's' in Chequers comes and goes, so presumably eithe. spelling must be acceptable. The tendency is for it to be dropped when followed by anothe 's', as in Street. On the left was The Malt Shovel. It may be Mr Smith in the pub doorway. The wheelbarrow was the property of Mrs Ashley's father, Mr Pegg, and he appears to be carryin a dog.

The "Old Chequer Inn,"

BULKINGTON.

J. Smith - - - - Proprietor.

EADIE & CO.'S ALES & STOUTS.

WINES AND SPIRITS.

CIGARS OF THE FINEST QUALITY

ACCOMMODATION FOR CYCLISTS.   GOOD STABLING.

AN ADVERTISEMENT FOR THE OLD CHEQUER INN, 1907. Eadie's Ales from Burton. Cycling wa something of a craze, hence its frequent mention in contemporary adverts.

CHEQUER STREET, 1920s. Perhaps twenty years later than the picture opposite but there is a marked change in fashion. The advertisement is for Rowntrees Cocoa. The other two offer property for sale in Bedworth.

CHEQUER STREET, 1981. The house behind the head of the little girl (third from left) in the top picture, is the one on the left of this picture. These were all weavers' homes. The building on the right is now a flower shop.

BARNACLE LANE, C. 1905. This early faded postcard has a lot of charm. The children play in the street unperturbed by traffic.

THE FARM AT THE TOP OF BARNACLE LANE, 1917. Farmed at this time by Mr Woodward. The brick wall on the extreme left is still there. It was also known as Well Green Farm.

VALUABLE FREEHOLD
PROPERTY
BULKINGTON.

TO BE SOLD BY AUCTION, BY

MESSRS. NIXON & SONS,

AT THE LORD NELSON INN, IN BULKINGTON,

ON WEDNESDAY, THE 27TH DAY OF JANUARY, 1875,

At Five o'Clock in the Afternoon, in the following or such other Lots as may be agreed upon at the time of Sale, and subject to the Conditions then to be produced.

LOT 1.—ALL THOSE

TWO WELL-BUILT MESSUAGES OR TENEMENTS,

With Large Weaver's Shop, situate in Church Street, Bulkington, now in the occupation of John Fulleylove and William Wilkes.

ALSO, ALL THAT

MESSUAGE OR DWELLING-HOUSE,

Containing Parlour. Living Room. Kitchen. Shop, Cellar. and Four Bed Rooms, together with the Two Wheelwright's Shops, Timber Yard. and Garden. situate at the back of the above, and now in the occupation of Mr. George Cuthbert, Junr.

Lot 2.—All that

PLOT OR PARCEL OF LAND,

Called " The Sandpit," situate in Bulkington aforesaid, and containing. by admeasurement 540 Square Yards. or thereabouts, now used as a Timber Yard, and also in the occupation of Mr. George Cuthbert, Junr.

Lot 3.—All those

THREE COTTAGES

Situate in a Yard at the back of the Crown Inn, in Bulkington, now in the respective occupations of William Hickinbottom. Sarah Shaw. and William Randle.

Lot 4.—All those

3 MESSUAGES OR TENEMENTS

Situate in Chequers Street in Bulkington aforesaid. now in the occupation of Thomas Pegg. one lately occupied by Thomas Goodyer. and the other unoccupied, together with the Weaver's Shop, Yard, and appurtenances thereto.

ALSO,

BLACKSMITH' SHOP

With Two Hearths, and Paint House, now unoccupied.

To View the above, apply to the Tenants; and, for further Particulars, to Mr.

AUCTION DETAILS, 1875. This is interesting for the detail it gives concerning properties in Chequer and Church Street. The 1871 census allows us to pin-point them precisely.

THE LORD NELSON INN, c. 1905, in Leicester Street, the venue for the auction shown on p. 39, thirty years earlier. It was the only three-storey building at the time on that side of the street, though there were two other pubs.

DR LIONEL ORTON with a pony and trap in about 1905. Based in Bedworth, Dr Orton had close contact with Bulkington, working from premises in the line shown here which were between The Chequers and Leicester Street.

LEICESTER STREET, 1905. This is a detail from a postcard by F.R. Jones of Nuneaton (see p. 42) and is a delightful view of the jumble of sizes and styles which made up Edwardian Leicester Street.

LEICESTER STREET, 1905. The full postcard by F.R. Jones reveals quite a wide street of largely early nineteenth-century buildings. At the top is, or was, The Square, scene of a recent acrimonious and enjoyable dispute.

LEICESTER STREET, 1950s, shows few changes over the fifty years. It is the last thirty which have transformed the village. The lady on the left is Mrs Hancocks. She is talking to the shopkeepers, Mr and Mrs Smart, who are outside their shop at No. 10. Riding the Francis Barnet motorcycle is Mr Friswell, a Bedworth builder.

BICKNELL'S CORNER, Leicester Street, c. 1930. So called because the Bicknell family owned the property. Imagine the present Co-op extending as far as Leicester Street and you have some idea of 'The Square' thus formed, with the White Lion at the eastern end. The property shown here stood approximately where the bottle bank now reposes.

LEICESTER STREET in the 1950s. Looking down the street, with Bicknell's shop on the left. The Rule and Compass is the extending gable on the right, with early and late nineteenth-century houses this side of it. The post office was in this line at one time.

The " Rule and Compass,"

~~⚜~~ BULKINGTON. ~~⚜~~

HENRY SUTTON - - - Proprietor.

Phillips and Marriott's

GOLD MEDAL - - -

PALE ALES & STOUT,

ON DRAUGHT AND IN BOTTLE.

WINES & SPIRITS of the Finest Quality.

Good Stabling and Draw-in Yard.

AN ADVERTISEMENT, 1907, for The Rule and Compass, Leicester Street, when Henry Sutton was proprietor.

THE RULE AND COMPASS, C. 1907. This superb photograph evokes the Edwardian atmosphere beautifully. Behind the shoulder of the man with the jug of ale is a poster in the window, announcing that the Anniversary Sermon was to be preached at the Congregational chapel by a Revd Bradley.

THE RULE AND COMPASS, C. 1930. Business was no doubt good enough for the pub to be rebuilt. It is now substantially the same as in 1930. In the distance is the former Home Farm, now being used as a haulage business by the Hughes family. A petrol advertisement is visible on the wall.

THE SQUARE, LEICESTER STREET, 1911. This was almost certainly the band which played from 9.00 till 10.00 on Thursday, 22 June, the coronation day of George V. There was a full programme of events in the village, from bell ringing at 8.00 a.m. to a bonfire at 10.00 p.m.

SERMONS PROCESSION in the early 1960s. This again shows The Square in use, as the vicar, Revd Hasted, leads the church procession round the village. The White Lion is on the right of the picture. Sermons Sunday in Bulkington parish church is the nearest Sunday to St James's Day, the saint to whom the church is dedicated.

BULKINGTON POST OFFICE, c. 1905. A lovely Edwardian view, with children obediently lined up – but not obstructing the shop – for the photograph. The post office moved several times from here.

ROWLEY, FAMILY BUTCHER, occupying the same site as the post office above. Later still it was used by the Birch family as a hardware store. Alison Evans wrote of observing frightened livestock being taken to the adjacent slaughterhouse in about 1910. Rowleys later set up a shop at Ryton in a building, now a house, overlooking the green.

White Lion Hotel,

BULKINGTON (THE FREE HOUSE).

F. WOODWARD - - Proprietor.

Splendid Wines, Spirits, & Ales.

F. W. ALSO CARRIES ON A - - -

BUTCHERING BUSINESS,

AND SUPPLIES JOINTS OF THE PRIMEST QUALITY·

AN ADVERTISEMENT FOR THE WHITE LION HOTEL, 1907. This pub still exists, tucked into the old square. There are many examples from the period of publicans having two jobs. Mr Woodward was also a butcher.

CUSTOMERS AT THE WHITE LION. The date is not known, but it appears to be from the inter-war period. The pub was headquarters for Bulkington Football Club.

JAMES WILSON.
Grocer & Baker,
LEICESTER STREET & SCHOOL ROAD.
BULKINGTON.

A CALENDAR for 1899, presented to customers by James Wilson, who kept the shop and bakery on the corner of Leicester Street and School Road. The original is a beautiful colour lithograph produced by Cooke of Leeds, and overprinted for shopkeepers all over the country.

CORONATION CELEBRATIONS, 22 June, 1911. The procession started at 2.30 p.m. Some of the little girls on the float are still living in the village. Holding the horse is young Master Page, one of the girls is his sister, and the boy on the trap is Cuthbert Larkin, later to become a headmaster.

WILSON'S SHOP, corner of Leicester Street and School Road, c. 1918. The road ended at the church gates. The tower can be seen on the right of the picture. On the extreme right is the Council Office when the village was administered by Rugby. Later this building became the Library.

THE CORNER OF LEICESTER STREET in the 1950s. Partly boarded up before demolition, the picture shows what a big corner building it was. In more recent times it was occupied by Furboroughs the butchers.

HOME FARM, School Road, c. 1909. The picture shows Mary Ashmore on the right, with two of her sisters. Mary Ashmore wrote delightful memories of her early days in the village which were published in local papers, and as two booklets published in the mid-1970s, one of them posthumously.

HOME FARM during demolition, c. 1980. The building had become almost hidden by more modern developments in School Road, but the picture shows how the farm was built in line with the church.

BULKINGTON C. OF E. SCHOOL, C. 1930. Originally built in 1861, costing £1,740, for 400 pupils to replace the earlier National School. It had a lasting good influence on village life.

SCHOOL CONVERSION. By the late 1960s the old school building had outgrown its usefulness and St James Middle School was built in Barbridge Road. The old school building was converted to a parish hall and the board indicates the amount raised, and the amount still to be raised, for conversion.

A BIRD'S EYE VIEW, actually from the vantage point of the church tower. It is looking down towards School Road and Leicester Street and dates from about 1930. The building at the bottom right was known as the Reading Room.

CHOOL ROAD, in the 1950s. The white line shows the road about to curve into Leicester Street. On the left, this side of the school, is the lovely chestnut tree which was held in great affection by villagers, until decay caused it to be felled in 1988. The tall building in the distance was the Co-op.

SCHOOL ROAD in the 1950s. A picture we can recognize! All the buildings on the right are still there although there has been redevelopment on the left. The first big house on the left belonged to the Woodward family.

SCHOOL ROAD, c. 1930. Again, a line of houses which is still there. Double-glazing salesmen have taken their toll, but the line is substantially the same.

SMITH'S EMPLOYEES. Behind the line of houses (see bottom of p. 54), and using some of them as offices, was Smith's hosiery factory, as well hidden a manufacturer as you could find. The firm is still there as part of the Scholl group.

TOM SMITH'S EMPLOYEES. Girls and women from the factory in formal pose during the early years of the century.

SCHOOL ROAD in the 1950s. The right-hand side is much the same, but there have been changes on the left. The Sandpits has now been developed, though the cluster of buildings including the Congregational chapel remains. Note the absence of traffic.

THE SANDPITS, c. 1907. A badly faded picture but few exist of the Sandpits. The large ground-floor window in one of the houses suggests its purpose for ribbon weaving.

THE SANDPITS in the 1950s. The distinctive brickwork, so common on buildings in the early nineteenth century. This includes the less usual (in Bulkington) top shops where large windows allowed good light for families to work on the looms. Top shops often incorporated machine-driven looms.

ARDEN ROAD, C. 1920. Arden Road was the eastern edge of Bulkington at this time. Beyond it were allotments and the distant place called Ryton.

THE POST OFFICE, c. 1930, Arden Road. Later the post office moved again to near its present site in School Road. All the houses in this picture remain.

ARDEN ROAD in the 1950s. The lack of traffic is marked, though the bus depot is visible at the end of the road.

ARDEN ROAD CORNER, in the 1950s showing the post-war development down Nuneaton Road, with the off-license on the corner. Originally it was a private house occupied by the Rook family.

ARDEN ROAD, c. 1915. The houses here were fairly new when these children posed on the verge. Behind the house on the right was a small weaving factory.

THE INTERIOR OF A WEAVING FACTORY, 1981. This little factory ceased production in the 1950s but some of the machinery stayed at roof level.

WEAVING WORKSHOP, 1981, Arden Road. The building took up most of the garden, and has now been demolished.

SECTION THREE

Ryton

NEW STREET in the 1950s. These council houses were built some sixty years ago, to the same design as those at the Bullring (pp. 12 and 15) and they made a link, with a new road, where before only a path existed, between Bulkington and Ryton. Even now, you confuse them at your peril.

RUGBY ROAD in the 1950s. Round the corner from New Street, where the police house stands, were these two cottages and small farm. On the left is June Knight's mother.

NEW INN, in the 1950s. This is one of the most popular photographs at slide shows, appealing to people for many reasons. The top shops indicate 1830s or 1840s ribbon weaving buildings, and the pub is actually the building between the two sets of top shops.

WITHYBROOK ROAD, c. 1907. Another line of weaving cottages, some of which remain, though there has been some redevelopment and in-filling in this line.

WITHYBROOK ROAD COTTAGE. The boy on a tricycle looks to be a robust Ryton youngster. It would be interesting to be able to identify him.

WITHYBROOK ROAD, c. 1930. The New Inn is in the distance, and Shilton Lane goes off to the left. There is no traffic at all.

MOTHER AND DAUGHTER (?) in Withybrook Road. There is a startling contrast in their hair styles. Again, sadly, no details have emerged as to their identity.

CLARICE LOVEITT standing in the door of her general store, 1920s. The building is now a private house, The Lilacs, on the corner near Ryton chapel, and Mr Clarke, who lives there with his family, is Clarice Loveitt's nephew.

RYTON METHODIST CHURCH, which opened in 1911, moving from an earlier chapel in Long Street (see p. 79). When Bulkington Methodist church closed in 1960 the members joined with Ryton.

THE INTERIOR, RYTON METHODIST CHURCH, at the first Harvest Festival held in the new building after it opened in 1911. As well as the produce, the lights are particularly impressive.

WOLVEY ROAD CORNER, before any of the more recent developments. The tiny corner building was once a blacksmith's shop.

WOLVEY ROAD, c.1908. This line of houses remains despite some individual redevelopment. The wide grass verge remains. The children were clearly fascinated and delighted to be included.

WOLVEY ROAD, c. 1908. A close up of part of the previous picture, itself a postcard. There is amazing detail, so it is possible to read on the canopy above the driver's head on the horse-drawn delivery vehicle that it came from the 'Stores, Abbey Street, Nuneaton'. It would almost certainly have belonged to Wilkinsons. In the background is a car.

LONG STREET, in the early 1960s. Almost all of old Ryton has gone. Fortunately a local enthusiast recorded many of the buildings before they disappeared. This one is by the junction with Wolvey Road. The gable on the right belongs to a building still there, looking over the green, and once Rowley's butchery. The rest have all gone.

MILNER'S FARM, June 1962. This was a huge farmhouse. All that remains now is the name of Milner Close. All the photographs between pages 70 and 75 were taken by local photographer Stanley Allcoat. There are many others by him elsewhere in the book.

LONG STREET, in the late 1950s. The house on the left is still there. Legend claims it was once a pub. Ryton was full of houses built behind and almost on top of each other in an extraordinary jumble. The frontage here is deceptive.

THE SAME LINE OF HOUSES AS ABOVE, but from the other end. Partial demolition revealed the jumble in all its glory. The large window on the right shouts weaving. The tiny house on the left seems to be one up, one down.

A TINY HOUSE IN LONG STREET, shown in its setting on p. 71, but here in greater detail.

ANOTHER TYPICAL PICTURE of an early nineteenth-century cottage used by Ryton weavers.

COTTAGES AT RYTON, February 1957. This line was opposite the Weavers Arms. These two pages show examples of the property in, and off, Long Street. Many have the distinctive 1830s and 1840s fashion for patterned brickwork. To contemporaries it must have been a time of considerable change.

MANY WEAVING COTTAGES were built in a line at right angles to the road. The cottages on p. 75 are good examples. They created a similar effect to the town courts and yards, though do not seem to have been quite so enclosed.

LARGE GROUND-FLOOR WINDOWS suggest the building was purpose-designed for a loom, often involving families and very young children in producing ribbon. This picture was taken in Long Street in February 1957.

SMALLER COTTAGES THAN SOME, but still in Ryton. Mr Doyle lived in one of these cottages.

A FARM BUILDING, RYTON, 1981. Down one of the many tracks off Long Street. It had fallen into neglect and has now disappeared.

A RENOVATED COTTAGE, IN RYTON. Set back from Long Street, this one has clung on as one of only a handful of the old cottages now remaining. It was Walter Elson's house when the picture was taken in 1961.

HALL GROUNDS FARM. This farmhouse is still there, at the far end of Long Street. The bow windows are likely to be later additions to the functional original. It would be interesting to discover the names of the subjects.

THIS FARMHOUSE appears to be later than many of the buildings, nearer to the turn of the century. Owned by the Elsons, it stood where Bramcote Close now is.

ANOTHER RYTON FARM. This was another example of a line at an angle to the road. Conditions seem hard at the time this picture was taken.

THE SAME BUILDING, but some decades later. Poor thatch has been replaced by corrugated iron, and whitewash applied to the walls. When this was taken it was owned by Mrs Bayliss. The date was 1961.

THE WESLEYAN CHAPEL, Long Street, c. 1904. A postcard by Jones and Bradbury of Nuneaton. In 1911 the chapel moved to its present site. The garden wall and step remain in front of the house called Bethel.

WEAVERS' COTTAGE, Wolvey Road. The only picture to emerge of a loom, visible through the door of the cottage. It is extraordinary that so few artefacts from a major form of employment have survived.

WEAVERS' COTTAGE. The building is still there, the last house on the left on Wolvey Road. The picture was taken in the early years of the century and we know that the lady holding the hand of the little boy was Miss Cross, a ribbon weaver.

Church

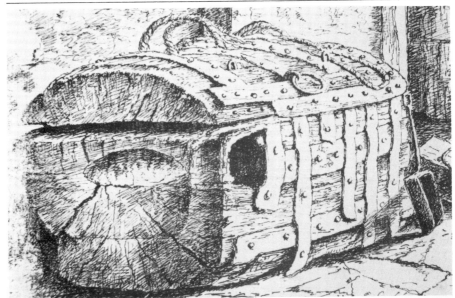

BULKINGTON PARISH CHEST. Originally all the parish documents were kept in the chest. This would include many documents now invaluable to local historians. County Record Offices now offer more reliable storage. This chest must have been enormous, and heavy. It appears to have been cut from one trunk.

PARISH CHURCH OF ST JAMES. This fine building is the oldest in the parish. Parts are thirteenth-century though evidence exists of an earlier Norman building. Most dates from 1200–1500, with restoration in the 1860s, and new work on the tower in 1907.

ULKINGTON VICARAGE, a large nineteenth-century building which cost a fortune to run and as sold to someone better able to pay the bills. The present, modern, vicarage is in the rounds of the old one. This picture dates from about 1930.

CHURCH ARMY VAN. This one was based in Coventry and did the rounds of local villages angelizing. Alison Evans wrote of seeing it in Exhall, with Mr Hudson in attendance, in 10. Here it was parked in Bulkington, but it is uncertain where.

THE FLOWER FESTIVAL, 1968. Over the years Bulkington has organized many flower festivals They are always well supported. This picture was taken of a festival on 25 May, 1968.

HARVEST FESTIVAL. Still a potent reminder of the conjunction of spiritual and physical man The wooden procession cross was in memory of Sam Carter and the candlesticks i memory of Alf Hancocks.

THE PARISH CHURCH FLOODLIT. The work was done under the expert guidance of Mr I.G. Morgan, who brought wide experience of floodlighting. He ran the village post office and has been a leading member, as has his wife, of the church. Many photographs have come from his collection. This was taken in the late 1950s. The floodlights were later stolen!

PRESENTATION TO REVD D.J. DINGLEY, 1959. He was vicar for over thirty years. The parish presented him with a silver tea set. On the left with the bouquet is Mrs Dingley; behind her is Mr Neale. The tea service is being presented by churchwardens Will Bason and Reg Green, who holds the framed inscription.

THE DEDICATION OF THE BELLS, 22 October, 1949. This was an imaginative response to th‹ problem of commemorating a war. On the front row are Mr Ashley, Mr Green, Revd Dingle‹ Mr Bason and Mr Hinde.

TO THE GLORY OF GOD

THE PRESENT RING OF SIX BELLS IN THIS TOWEF
WAS INCREASED TO EIGHT IN 1949 AS A MEMORIAL
THE TREBLE BELL DEDICATED TO THE MEN OF THI
PARISH WHO GAVE THEIR LIVES. THE SECOND BEL
AS A THANK OFFERING FOR THE SAFE RETURN
OF THOSE WHO SERVED.   1939 – 1945.

REV. J.H. DINGLEY, L.D.,   VICAR
W.W. BASON)   CHURCH
R.H. GREEN)   WARDENS

THE PLAQUE IN THE CHURCH explaining the reason for the installation of two additional bells i 1949.

SERMONS SUNDAY. The last leg of the procession has brought them up Church Street. Alf Hinde (his house is in the background) leads the choir and churchwardens back to church.

THE INDUCTION OF REVD J. HASTED, 1959. Church officials in this picture are Alan Gray, Gordon Morgan, Revd Cuthbert Bardsley (Bishop of Coventry), Will Bason, Revd Hasted, Mr Campling and Mr Slingsby.

CONFIRMATION CANDIDATES. This delightful picture was taken the year Jane Morgan was confirmed. She is on the left, c. 1963.

NATIVITY PLAY. No doubt many of these youngsters will have children of their own, nearly thirty years on, appearing in nativity plays in the village! Taken in the late 1960s.

DOROTHY ALDRIDGE, a life-long active member of the church, in the choir and as organist. She is shown here with choristers Tony Crowther and Maurice Randall, in the 1930s.

A POSTCARD VIEW OF ST JAMES, c. 1904, showing it before the tower was altered, and when it was surrounded by more magnificent trees.

89

AN AERIAL VIEW of the early 1960s, showing the church at the centre, appropriately since the picture was used on the cover of the parish magazine. The open land to the west and north emphasize how the church was once at the north end of a village largely encircled by Leicester Street, Chequer Street and Church Street.

AN AERIAL VIEW in the 1970s, after the School Road – Bedworth Road extension, which altered the geometry of the village. The different Ryton community is clear, as are the post-war developments alongside Nuneaton Road. Medieval open field strips are visible under the recreation ground.

School

BULKINGTON C. OF E. SCHOOL in the early years of the century. Several of these pictures have survived, from different years. This one is unusual in that some pupils are sitting, even standing, on the school wall – a rare relaxation of rules!

SCHOOL HOUSE, BULKINGTON. The house stood at the side of the school, on the site of the present library. Among headteachers to live there were Mr Winterton, Mr Larkin and Mr Ward.

THOMAS AND ESTHER WINTERTON on their wedding picture in 1860. Mr Winterton came as first headteacher, with his wife as governess, of the new school in 1862. It was a hard time for the village. The ribbon trade had collapsed and families were emigrating. In 1861 there were eighty-three vacant houses in the parish.

THE WINTERTON FAMILY. They had five sons and a daughter (another died in infancy). All distinguished themselves as clergy and teachers, at home and abroad.

MR AND MRS WINTERTON. For some thirty-six years they ran the school. A contemporary report says 'the big rough lads, accustomed to have matters their own way, gradually yielded to the superior will, and were eventually effectively quelled'. The school won glowing reports from an HMI and influenced generations of pupils.

MR WINTERTON and a somewhat subdued class pose sometime in the 1890s.

'OUNGER CHILDREN in the Infant department pose for their class, or standard, picture before he First World War.

MR LARKIN AND STAFF C. 1907. Mr Larkin followed Winterton as head. He too maintained high standards. On the back row are Miss Sage, Mr Larkin and Mr Barnet. In front are Mrs Winterton (née Farndon) and Marie, Mrs Larkin and Gwen, Miss Woodward, Miss Poole and Miss Hurley.

MR LARKIN AND A CLASS, about the same year, C. 1908.

AN INFANT CLASS in the new school for the Infant department which opened in 1939. This picture dates from c. 1948 and the teacher is May Dawkins, with her helper Mrs Carvell.

INFANT SCHOOL from the same post-war period. Mrs Elson is on the left, Mrs Breedon on the right.

MRS HARE AND HER CLASS in the Infant department c. 1948/9. The class seems eager to learn, and no doubt they were.

MRS FROST AND HER CLASS at Bulkington C. of E. School in 1942/3. These children are now comfortably into their fifties!

Village Life in Bulkington and Ryton

Œ. ℟.
Coronation of Edward VII.

Admit *Mr G Legg*

☞ TO ❀| **DINNER** |❀

AT THE

National Schools, Bulkington,
At 1 o'clock on Thursday, June 26th, 1902.

GOD SAVE THE KING.

Born 1841, Crowned 1902.

CORONATION DINNER, 1902. Most communities arrange special events for royal occasions and the coronation of Edward VII, after Victoria's long reign, was certainly marked in this area.

DOROTHY ALDRIDGE, née Harrison, at one of the festivities held in the village before the First World War. It is a really charming picture.

PRESENTATION TO LADY NEWDEGATE by a delightful little girl, c. 1950. Also in the picture are the Revd and Mrs Dingley, and Reg Green.

SILVER JUBILEE, 1935. Mr Bason, in straw hat, stands near the table laden with commemorative mugs.

BULKINGTON CHILDREN. Difficult to date or place, but outside a shop, perhaps in the 1930s. Worth printing for some of the marvellously expressive faces.

AN OVER SIXTIES OUTING. One of many, this was organized by the War Memorial Club.

RYTON RESIDENTS in some sort of fancy dress for a carnival or fête, before the First World War. They are Ruby, Clarice and Mildred Loveitt and their mother. Mildred died, aged 86, in 1987.

A TEA PARTY AT RYTON, venue and occasion unknown, but it is clearly an important occasion with all in their best clothes, either side of a gleaming tea urn. Probably c. 1910.

MRS HARRISON outside her house in Church Street, when an elderly lady. She was the sister of Frederick Benn, proprietor of the Crown (see p. 26).

MR AND MRS LOVETT, in formal pose for Mr Chettle of Nuneaton. They were the great grandparents of Mr Clarke, who loaned the photograph. Mary Ashmore's grandfather hired a William Loveitt of Ryton as a cow-lad in the 1840s for an annual wage of £5.

CARNIVAL CAPERS, C. 1949. This fancy dress parade was held in the grounds of Weston Hall. There will be many who recognize themselves here.

THE REVD HASTED with mothers and children in the old school building, around 1960.

AN EARLY CRICKET TEAM. We think this team contains cricketing names like Bolsworth, Smith, Pegg, Ashley, Barratt and Newman, but would welcome details.

A PRE-WAR FOOTBALL SQUAD. Again the names are unknown. There are many photographs around of sporting teams over many years. This is a token sample.

SCOUTING IN BULKINGTON. Again, there are many scouting pictures, and the two here are a token sample of the contribution scouting has made to village life.

SCOUT CAMP. Two leaders take time off for a pipe. Mr Hinde, among all his other activities, was a leading scouting enthusiast for many years.

A MUSICIAN OUTSIDE THE READING ROOM. This was off Church Street. Date and name unknown. There is a long and distinguished musical tradition in Bulkington.

BULKINGTON PARISH BAND. The date is uncertain. The brass bands in the area, especially the Bulkington Silver Band, have long histories and excellent traditions which rival many of the better known national bands.

A MARCHING BAND, but date and details are unknown. It looks as if the picture is from the First World War period.

THE VICARAGE GARDEN PARTY, 1925. All the ladies dressed up and they include Sally White, Kitty Farndon, Agnes Record, Hilda Record, Mrs Newcombe, Dorothy Aldridge, Laura Benn, Mrs Smith and Florrie Warden.

CONCERT PARTIES AND PLAYS were amazingly successful and popular in the first quarter of the century. The guiding force seems to have been Will Bason who gathered fellow enthusiasts and amused and entertained the village for years. This one appears to be First World War period and the poster says 'Lloyd George – People's Pet'.

OPERETTA AT BULKINGTON SCHOOL, 1912, when Mr Bason and his players performed 'Gipsy Queen'.

BULKINGTON HOME GUARD used to meet at Weston Hall. Some sixty of them were photographed here towards the end of the war.

VICTORY CELEBRATION TEA, 1945. This was held at the British Legion Club, and many of the youngsters here are still in the village, though beginning to show their years!

CORONATION DAY, 2 June 1953. Bulkington had wonderful floats and processions. On these two pages are four of the many photographs taken that day. Many readers will recognize themselves.

CORONATION DAY, June 1953. The pram race, proving that adults are just grown-up kids. Note the coats and headscarves. It rained on 2 June.

CHILDREN AS ROSES ON CORONATION DAY 1953. Presumably we admire the petals rather than the thorns. It is a delightful picture.

THE RURAL FLOAT, at the coronation, 1953, complete with sheep.

HARVEST SUPPER, C. 1960. During the time of Revd Hasted, and afterwards, Mrs Morgan and her committee organized huge and hugely successful harvest suppers. Over 200 used to sit down to a meal in the old school.

HARVEST SUPPER. This, and the picture above, contain many familiar faces.

THE WAR MEMORIAL CLUB. They also arranged dinners and this picture shows the mayor and honoured guests at a dinner in the 1960s.

YOUNG WIVES FELLOWSHIP, the committee which organized the harvest suppers in the early 1960s. The ladies are Mrs Hancock, Mrs Barratt, Mrs Bowns, Mrs Kendall, Mrs Morgan, Mrs Sephton, Mrs Jones and Mrs Essex.

RIBBON WEAVING LOOM, borrowed from Coventry Museum for the Bulkington Through The Ages Exhibition in 1981. Many photographs in this book came from the exhibition. The village traditionally earned its living from farming and weaving, so these pictures are appropriate symbols. The ribbons behind the loom were produced locally.

THE FARNDONS were bakers and farmers, and had a strong influence in the village. The loaf was baked specially for the Exhibition.

Shilton and Ansty Streets and Buildings

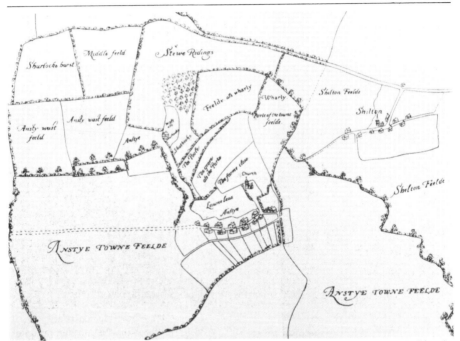

AN EARLY MAP OF ANSTY AND SHILTON, thought to date from 1587. The site occupied by the cottages, in Main Road, Ansty, near the church seems to be the original village. The coming of the canal extended the village towards Coventry.

THE ROAD TO BULKINGTON out of Shilton, c. 1907. This is a very agricultural scene. Many of the cottages remain.

A COMPOSITE POSTCARD OF SHILTON, c. 1925. Four fifths of this show church-related views. Whether Shilton, even in 1925, was that committed to Anglicanism, must remain doubtful.

THE CENTRE OF SHILTON, c. 1907. Now a busy little junction, though it still seems odd to have traffic lights there.

THE SCHOOL AND VILLAGE, c.1905. The school served Ansty as well and was a unifying force. They have been legally one parish for over a century and there seems less rivalry between Ansty and Shilton than between Bulkington and Ryton.

SHILTON FROM THE CHURCH TOWER. This comes from a photograph by Bleasdale of Nuneaton, c. 1905. There was some weaving here but not on the scale that changed the face of Bulkington. Shilton and Ansty remained rooted in farming but like all villages are now largely dormitories.

A CLOSE UP OF CHILDREN FROM SHILTON SCHOOL. Imagine the press reaction if today you encouraged a class of children to stand across the road to have their photograph taken! In 1907 roads could safely be playgrounds.

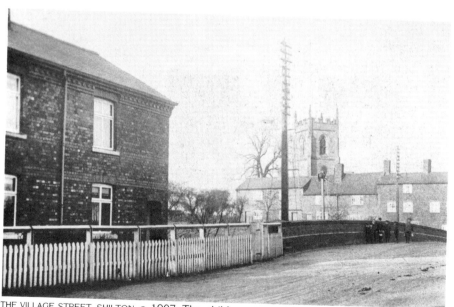

THE VILLAGE STREET, SHILTON, c. 1907. The children are standing on the railway bridge. The distant buildings suggest rather more than farming cottages. The postcard was one of many by Ratledge of Rugby.

SHILTON HOUSE, C. 1925. One of a series of postcards by Teesee. It is a fine-looking building and clearly impressed the card producer since he photographed the rear as well.

Rockery, Shilton House.

SHILTON HOUSE AND ROCKERY, C. 1925. At one time it was owned by Mrs Oliver Bellasis, who moved here after leaving Ansty Hall.

SHILTON VICARAGE, C. 1925. Built on the outskirts of the village, on the way to Barnacle. During the time of Revd Victor Bennett there was ferocious village dispute, which delighted the press, about road widening by the church. These ghosts are best left undisturbed.

ENGINE 45672 and train photographed by Mr John Robinson at Nettle Hill cutting by Holly Hill Bridge, near Shilton station.

SHILTON STATION, c. 1907. Between the main platforms was the ungainly passenger bridge which stood up against the road bridge behind it.

SHILTON STATION. By now there was a more elaborate waiting room than in 1907. A local steam train approaches the platform and a porter is preparing to load milk churns. On the right is a half-timbered barn of some antiquity.

ANSTY HALL, C. 1908. Looking from the canal bridge across the fields to the hall at the top of the rise. Still surrounded by lofty trees, it looks particularly magnificent in autumn.

AN ENGRAVING OF ANSTY HALL. Richard Tayler lived many years in Ansty. He died in 1676 and was succeeded by his son Edward, who pulled down the old manor house and built the present hall, though not to its present size, in 1678. It remained in the family until the death of a later Edward Tayler in 1799.

ANSTY HALL, C. 1925. The rear of the Hall shows clearly the later additions of a top storey and recessed wings. In 1799 Simon Adams (Edward Tayler's nephew) inherited the hall and it remained in the direct line until 1956. Since then it has passed through various branches of the family until it was sold in 1987 and is now a hotel.

THE LODGE AND HERMITAGE, C. 1907. The Hermitage is still on the curve of the road but the lodge was demolished in the early 1950s. It was built in the 1840s on the site of an old farm which was used as a vicarage by Revd T.C. Adams.

ANSTY HALL LODGE, c. 1907. Built in the 1840s it became the Dower House for the hall. Villagers recollect that the Bush family lived there from the 1920s. After their deaths in the 1940s it remained empty. A secret room was found during demolition, they say.

ANSTY CHURCH, c. 1925. From an attractive postcard which shows a well-kempt churchyard and surroundings.

OLD CHURCH, ANSTY. This was largely thirteenth and fourteenth-century, with alterations made in the seventeenth century. Major repairs were carried out by Revd T.C. Adams, vicar from 1809–51.

CHURCH AND STEEPLE. In December 1854 Major-General Henry Adams of Ansty Hall died, aged forty-nine, of wounds sustained at the Battle of Inkerman. In 1856 his widow commissioned the important architect Sir Gilbert Scott to build a spire in memory of her husband. In 1876 Scott carried out a further restoration of the church.

COTTAGES, MAIN ROAD, ANSTY, C. 1907. The nearest ones seem more recent than the thatched ones, but may themselves be replacements for earlier cottages. A picture of great charm, helped by the knowledge that it still looks almost the same.

AN AERIAL VIEW in the 1970s of the same cottages. At the top of the picture is the Oxford Canal.

THE COTTAGE OPPOSITE THE CROWN, C. 1907. It appears to be early nineteenth-century and the far window (clearer in top picture opposite) appears to be a bricked-up weavers' window. The little girls outside are Florence and May Dyson. Their parents owned the cottage.

THE COTTAGE OPPOSITE THE CROWN, 25 April, 1908. The men outside are passers-by, probably amazed at a photographer in the snow. There were freak snow storms all over England that weekend. The 25th was a Saturday and it snowed on and off all day (see pp. 132 and 136).

HE CROWN INN, ANSTY, c. 1907. The proprietors had been the Adcock family from the mid-1800s. In 1892 Thomas and Jane Webb became tenants and stayed until the early 900s when May Adcock took over. Later hosts were the Butlers, who had performed in music and opera all over the world, before coming to Ansty.

HOME FARM, 25 April, 1908. Photographs all over the country recorded the unusual snow on this Saturday in spring. We know its effect locally from the journal kept by Alison Evans of Bedworth.

HOME FARM, 26 April, 1908. After the freak snow it was an even greater surprise that by Sunday 26th snow lay a foot deep. Few Ansty people travelled far that day. It was said to be the deepest snow in parts for forty years.

A WORKING BUTTY on the Oxford Canal near Ansty, probably during the 1930s.

HOME FARM, aerial view of the 1960s. The land here has been farmed by the Payne family for many years.

CANALSIDE SHOP AND COTTAGE, Ansty. The shop has gone and is now a house. At one time Mrs Veasey lived there, though the property belonged to Ansty Hall.

WORKING CANAL BOATS, C. 1907. This barge, *Elizabeth*, is well-loaded and is worked by John Grantham of Banbury. It is a fascinating picture.

A COTTAGE IN ANSTY, a few yards from the canal (see bottom left of picture on p. 133), showing Lucy Hollis, aged two, holding hands with her father Joshua Hollis outside their cottage.

CANALSIDE COTTAGES, actually at right angles to the canal and visible from the rear on the picture opposite. Mr Edward Goodburn is standing outside, in 1907.

CANALSIDE COTTAGES, 25 April, 1908. Another in the series taken by the intrepid snow photographer that weekend. Ansty was often spelt with an 'e' in earlier years.

CANALSIDE COTTAGES, as above, but taken eighty years to the day later, on 25 April 1988, as a deliberate contribution to this book! The camera here was a few feet nearer the canal because the leaves and branches of the chestnut tree (a sapling above) now obscure the view.

OXFORD CANAL, ANSTY, 1907. The windmill has gone but older traces of man's mark are harder to eradicate. On the left are the ridge and furrow lines from Ansty's Town Field, the remains of medieval strip farming.

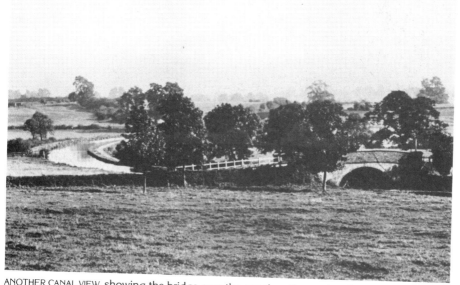

ANOTHER CANAL VIEW, showing the bridge over the canal on the road to Coombe. The picture dates from 1925.

THE APPROACH TO THE CANAL BRIDGE, c. 1910. Six groups pose for the photograph in these days when the canal was probably busier than the road. The groups could well include Veaseys and Aldridges.

THE ROAD TO THE CANAL BRIDGE, 1907. The old bridge is visible in both these pictures. The wider, newer one appears overleaf. The house on the left remains.

THE ALDRIDGE FAMILY, C. 1907 outside their house, The first in The Row leading to the canal.

THE JUNCTION WITH GROVE ROAD. The house in the foreground is still there and was owned in the 1920s by Mr and Mrs Eden. Just behind the house is a narrow lane of houses leading to the canal.

A MODERN VIEW from the 1950s of the approach to Ansty from Coventry. There are now more houses on the right.

BROOK COTTAGES, 1907. Two cottages, inhabited before the war by Mrs Lucas and Bernard Veasey. Now converted into very attractive houses.

Village Life in Ansty and Shilton

COMMEMORATIVE CHINA for the coronation of Edward VII on 26 June, 1902. The old, alternative spelling of Anstey prevails here. One wonders how many sets were produced and how many remain.

VILLAGE OUTING? Children in Sunday best, one with a bouquet, line up in front of Hollis's cottage, opposite Home Farm. But what for? They are accompanied by four adults.

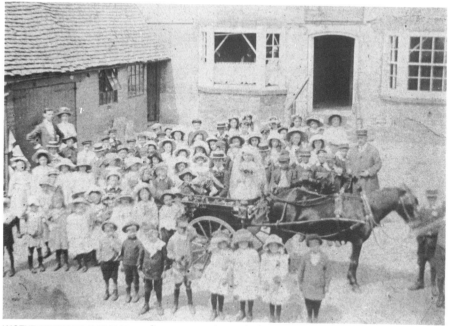

ANOTHER PROBLEM PHOTOGRAPH. It appears to be early (c. 1900) and a May Day celebration or procession, but the pub does not look like the front of the Crown.

SHILTON SCHOOL SERVED BOTH VILLAGES and many pictures survive from earlier years. The building dates from 1848, with later additions. This picture shows the cast of the annual school concert in 1925.

WEDDING GROUP. The wedding of Edith Taylor to Charles Arthur Thompson at Ansty church was followed by a reception at Shilton school on 15 June 1933.

ARMISTICE SUNDAY. Ex-servicemen marched from Shilton school to the church. In this picture are Mr R. Eden, Mr Hughes and Mr A. James.

SHILTON'S SWIMMING POOL is actually the school's pool, but it is unusual for a small rural school to have one. It was built in 1957 and is in use here a few years later.

SILVER JUBILEE. 1935. Village children at the fête held to celebrate. The attractive girl in the middle is Cynthia Anderton.

SILVER JUBILEE, 1935. The fête included a fancy dress parade. Here we see parish clerk Norman Ashman playing himself, with Alvan (a herald), Joy (baby bunting) and Milly (Britannia) Rigby.

REPOSE IN OLD AGE. This delightful picture shows Mrs Mary Veasey, who at one time was the oldest resident in Ansty.

OLD AGE HAD ITS OWN FORM OF DRESS in earlier years, with bonnets and shawls. This elderly Ansty resident was Mrs Mary Ann Goodburn.

SARAH BOLTON OF SHILTON. This extraordinary picture was taken in 1925 when Mrs Bolton wa 100. She entertained 200 children at a party. She never saw the sea and lived all her life i Shilton. With her is her son Josiah, daughter Mrs Thomas Coling, and great-grandso Harold Budrick.

THE ATHERSTONE HUNT meeting at Ansty Hall sometime in the mid-1960s.

THE ARCHERY CLUB had many supporters in both villages over a long period, extending until after the last war.

THE ARCHERY CLUB, First-World-War period. We know some of the names. Back row: Bill Brown, Harry Rowe, Revd Pyemont, -?-, -?-, Arthur Goodburn, Harry Stanley. Front row Harry Bosworth, Joe Dyson, -?-, -?-, Harry Goodburn.

THE ARCHERY CLUB, perhaps fifteen to twenty years later, with some of the same names. The are: Joe Dyson, Harry Bosworth, Harry Goodburn, Harry Bragg, Charlie Ryton, Charlie Watts Seated are Mr Thomas and Harry Stanley.

A FAMILY GROUP before the Second World War – the Paynes from Home Farm. Mrs Payne with daughters Eva (left) and Cissie.

THE CHURCH FÊTE AT ANSTY HALL in the 1950s. Well-hidden at the back are, from left to right, Mr Tustin, Mr Stopford-Adams and Mr Woolcombe-Adams. Middle row: Mrs Sansom, Mrs Payne, Mrs Ginns, Miss Grindal, Miss Timms, Miss Gardner, Mrs Tustin, Mrs Robinson, Mrs Simm, Revd Bennett, Mrs Rigby. Front row: Miss Smith, Mrs Rice, Mrs Woolcombe-Adams, Mrs Stopford-Adams.

RETIREMENT GIFT to Canon Harold Smith presented after fifty years in the ministry, twenty-five of them in Ansty and Shilton. He is accompanied by his daughter and was presented with a wallet and cheque for £116 by verger Harry Stanley.

WOMEN'S INSTITUTE from the local area on a visit to what appears to be Coventry and seems to date from the 1950s.

THIS LITTLE GIRL with her doll was taken many years ago when Lucy Hemmings was five.

ANSTY PANTOMINE. This pre-war jollity was a production of *Cinderella*. It was written and directed by Mr L. Anderton (second left, back row). They used to tour local villages to raise money to maintain the village hall.

GENTILITY IN ANSTY. This lovely photograph is of a family tea, beautifully posed in a garden.

ANSTY AND SHILTON BROWNIES. They were lead by Mrs Knight and Miss Bush. The local group started in the early 1930s and finished during the war. They met at Shilton school and the Lodge at Ansty, where this picture was taken.

THE CONTRAST BETWEEN THESE TWO PICTURES says much about social life in the last two generations. Mr Albert Heath is shown here playing an organ in pre-television days when communities made their own amusements. He lived from 1866 to 1946.

WITH TELEVISION THE WORLD VISITS YOUR SITTING ROOM and here Albert Heath's daughter, Mrs Milly Rigby, watches an early BBC programme introduced by Sylvia Peters.

WITH THE ARRIVAL OF VEHICLES villages lost their isolation and some of their cohesiveness. Vehicles and war broadened the horizons of many men, assuming they survived. This picture is not of Ansty, but it shows Albert Heath again (on the right) caught up in the turmoil of the First World War, in the Medical Corps.

CHARABANC OUTINGS were popular after the First World War since most people had no access to cars. This was the Ansty and Shilton Mothers' Union outing in 1926.

CHANGING TIMES MADE PEOPLE WANT CARS. This one was bought by the Payne family in the 1920s. It is parked outside Home Farm.

A MACABRE INTEREST is always taken in accidents. This bus came off the road at Cross Gates Field, Ansty one day in the 1920s.

HAYMAKING in the 1920s. Pictures of farming are not common because farmers were too busy to bother, but these two capture the atmosphere well.

THE ROOFTOPS OF HOME FARM and other cottages can be seen in the distance. The haymaking was in Lady Craft Field, Ansty.

A PRIZE BEAST, photographed with its owner, farmer Sam Taylor from Noon Hill Farm, at the top of Grove Road, by an itinerant photographer.

A FAMILY PICNIC for the Heaths. Money was often scarce for most families before the war, but picnics could be fun and inexpensive in a local field. Here were, from left to right: a family friend, Maud Heath, George Tyrrell, Emily Heath, Nellie Heath, Evelyn Heath, Milly Rigby, and her little daughter Milly.

ACKNOWLEDGEMENTS

I am most indebted to May Dawkins and Mary Goodland for their help, support, and great enthusiasm. Particular thanks go to all those who lent photographs for the 1981 Exhibition. At the time I did not record them as I copied their pictures. I can only apologize to those several people who will see their pictures in the book and look in vain for an acknowledgement. There has been much kindness and support for the project over several years from people with an interest in Bulkington – people like Peter Wyman, Mr and Mrs Wilkins, Derek and Dorothy Thomas, Ralph Barratt and others. I have had tremendous help and support from Gordon Morgan. His pictures relating to church events are outstanding and he has an infectious enthusiasm and memory for Bulkington matters.

Bulkington owes a great debt of gratitude to the skills of Stanley Allcoat. He is a photographer of rare talent and the section on Ryton is almost entirely made up of his pictures from the late 1950s and early 1960s. It is salutary to think that without his interest and skill the majority of Ryton would have passed unrecorded.

There have been contributions and help over ten years from all the following:
the late Geoff Edmands ● Miss Smith (Rugby Road) ● Mrs Ashley
Alan Robinson ● Dorothy Blundred ● the *Bedworth Echo* ● Mrs Turner
the late Reg Green ● Mr Taylor (Old Chequers) ● Mrs Spencer
Mrs Rosemary Hutt ● Gordon Morgan ● May Dawkins ● Mrs Sheila Gernon
Mrs Joan Uren ● Michael Smith ● Stanley Allcoat ● Ralph James
Stan and Margaret Clarke ● Mrs W. White ● Dorothy Aldridge ● Darrell Buckley
Reg Neale ● British Legion ● Fred Phillips ● Mrs A. Jones ● Roger Jones
Lynda Carnes.

Specifically for help with the Ansty and Shilton sections Mary received help from
Mr and Mrs Anderton
Mrs Buckland ● Mrs Hemmings ● Mr and Mrs Hinde ● Mr G. Payne
Mr and Mrs Pope ● Mr and Mrs Robertson ● Mr J. Robinson ● Mrs L. Robinson
Mr and Mrs Simms ● Mr and Mrs Simpson ● Mr Stopford-Adams
Mr and Mrs Willey ● Mrs Woolcombe-Adams ● Mr and Mrs Wright.

Finally, the postcard producers over ninety years who recorded local views. Ernest Ratledge, trading as Express Photo Co. in Rugby produced numerous cards of Ansty and some of Bulkington and Shilton. All date from about 1907 and most show views we would simply not have without his work. Sadly his darkroom skills were such that many cards are badly faded. There were other anonymous producers, some of whose work is excellent, and usually pre-1910. The Teesee Company produced very good quality cards of Shilton and Ansty in the mid-1920s, and an anonymous firm produced some excellent cards of Bulkington in about 1930 which turn up regularly, both in a machine-printed edition and a real photograph set. In the 1950s Gordon Morgan sold a set of contemporary cards from the post office. Two Nuneaton men produced cards before 1910: Bleasdale had a set of Shilton cards produced and F.R. Jones produced the card used for the cover of this book.